Here a Little Child I Stand
Satomi Ichikawa

Poems of Prayer and Praise for Children
Chosen by
Cynthia Mitchell

Philomel Books
New York

*The compiler, illustrator and publishers would like
to thank the following for permission to reproduce the poems in this book:*

Curtis Brown Ltd for "Morning Prayer," copyright © 1961, 1962 by Ogden Nash; A R Mowbray & Co Ltd for "God of All Our Cities" from *God of All Things* by Joan Gale Thomas; Oxford University Press for "A Morning Song" from *The Children's Bells* by Eleanor Farjeon; "The Prayer of the Little Ducks" from *Prayers From the Ark* by Carmen Bernos de Gasztold, translated by Rumer Godden, copyright 1947, 1955 Editions de Cloitre, English text copyright © 1962 by Rumer Godden, reprinted by permission of Viking Penguin Inc; Gyldendal, Copenhagen, for "The Kayak Paddler's Joy at the Weather," traditional Eskimo poem translated by William Thelbitzer from *The Unwritten Song* (Macmillan, 1966); Ian McDonald for "Georgetown Children"; The Society of Authors as the literary representative of the Estate of Cecil Roberts for "Prayer for the Pilot"; Lescher and Lescher Ltd for "My Bath," copyright © 1974 by Madeleine L'Engle; "Tambourines" from *Selected Poems of Langston Hughes,* copyright © 1959 by Langston Hughes, reprinted by permission of Alfred A. Knopf, Inc; Wheelwright Museum of the American Indian for "Navajo Creation Myth" by Hasteen Klah, recorded by Mary Cabot Wheelwright; "Evening Hymn" from *Song in the Meadow* by Elizabeth Madox Roberts, copyright 1940 by Elizabeth Madox Roberts, copyright renewed © 1967 by Ivor S Roberts, reprinted by permission of Viking Penguin Inc; "Sleep, Sleep" (An African Lullaby) from *My Book House,* © United Educators, Inc; "Sing a Song of People" from *The Life I Live* by Lois Lenski, reprinted by permission of Lois Lenski Covey Foundation.

First published in the United States of America in 1985
by Philomel Books, a division of The Putnam Publishing Group,
51 Madison Avenue, New York, NY 10010. First published
1985 by William Heinemann Ltd., London, England.

Library of Congress Cataloging in Publication Data

Ichikawa, Satomi.   Here a little child I stand.
Summary: A selection of religious poems from the Upanishads,
the Old Testament, and the likes of Langston Hughes, Ogden Nash,
and Robert Herrick.   1. Religious poetry. 2. Children—Prayer books
and devotions—English.   3. Children's poetry. {1. Religious
poetry.   2. Poetry—Collections} I. Mitchell, Cynthia.
II title. PN6110.R4I25   1985   808.81   85-3450
ISBN 0-399-21244-2

PRINTED IN THE UNITED KINGDOM.

To my Grandmother
from Satomi

The moon shines bright,
The stars give light
Before the break of day;
God bless you all
Both great and small
And send you a joyful day.

TRADITIONAL

Now another day is breaking,
Sleep was sweet and so is waking,
Dear Lord, I promised you last night
Never again to sulk or fight.
Such vows are easier to keep
When a child is sound asleep.
Today, O Lord, for your dear sake,
I'll try to keep them when awake.

OGDEN NASH

Here a little child I stand,
Heaving up my either hand;
Cold as paddocks* though they be,
Here I lift them up to thee,
For a benison to fall
On our meat, and on us all.

ROBERT HERRICK   *toads

Dear Father,
  hear and bless
Thy beasts
  and singing birds:
And guard
  with tenderness
Small things
  that have no words.

ANONYMOUS

Glory be to that God who is in the fire,
Who is in the waters,
Who is in plants and in trees,
Who is in all things in this vast creation.
Unto that Spirit be glory and glory.

HINDU   From the SVETASVATARA UPANISHAD

God of all our cities
Each alley, street and square,
Pray look down on every house
And bless the people there.

JOAN GALE THOMAS

Morning has broken
Like the first morning,
Blackbird has spoken
Like the first bird.
Praise for the singing!
Praise for the morning!
Praise for them springing
Fresh from the Word!

ELEANOR FARJEON

Dear God,
give us a flood of water.
Let it rain tomorrow and always.
Give us plenty of little slugs
and other luscious things to eat.
Protect all folk who quack
and everyone who knows how to swim.
                                        Amen

CARMEN BERNOS DE GASZTOLD
(translated by Rumer Godden)

Thank God for sleep in the long quiet night,
    For the clear day calling through the little leaded panes,
For the shining well-water and the warm golden light,
    And the paths washed white by singing rains.

For the treasure of the garden, the gilly-flowers of gold,
    The prouder petalled tulips, the primrose full of spring,
For the crowded orchard boughs, and the swelling buds that hold
    A yet unwoven wonder, to Thee our praise we bring.

Thank God for good bread, for the honey in the comb,
    For the brown-shelled eggs, for the clustered blossom set
Beyond the open window in a pink and cloudy foam,
    For the laughing loves among the branches set.

For earth's little secret and innumerable ways,
    For the carol and the colour, Lord, we bring
What things may be of thanks, and that Thou has lent our days
    Eyes to see and ears to hear and lips to sing.

JOHN DRINKWATER

When I'm out of the house in the open, I feel joy.
When I get out on the sea on hap-hazard, I feel joy.
If it is really fine weather, I feel joy.
If the sky really clears nicely, I feel joy.
May it continue thus for the good of my sealing!
May it continue thus for the good of my hunting!
May it continue thus for the good of my singing match!
May it continue thus for the good of my drum-song!

TRADITIONAL ESKIMO
(translated by William Thelbitzer)

Under the soursop silver-leaf tree
The High School children play skip-and-free:

Sun burning down like a fire ball.
Watch the children before school call.

Laugh in their gay time, laughter rich,
Jump the jack, bring marble pitch.

Black child, yellow child, brown child, white,
They are all the same if you looking right.

The biggest thing in life could be
Watching the children play skip-and-free.

IAN MCDONALD (GUYANA)

For lo, the winter is past,
The rain is over and gone;
The flowers appear on the earth;
The time of the singing of birds is come,
And the voice of the turtle
    Is heard in our land;
The fig tree putteth forth her green figs,
And the vines with the tender grapes
    Give a good smell.

SONG OF SOLOMON
OLD TESTAMENT

Lord of Sea and Earth and Air,
Listen to the pilot's prayer –
Send him wind that's steady and strong,
Grant that his engine sings the song
Of flawless tone, by which he knows
It shall not fail him where he goes;
Landing, gliding, in curve, half-roll –
Grant him, O Lord, a full control,
That he may learn in heights of Heaven
The rapture altitude has given,
That he shall know the joy they feel
Who ride Thy realms on birds of steel.

CECIL ROBERTS

My bath is the ocean
and I am a continent
with hills and valleys
and earthquakes and storms.
I put the two mountain peaks of my knees
under water and bring them up again.

Our earth was like that –
great churnings and splashings,
and continents appearing and disappearing.

Only you, O God, know about it all,
and understand, and take care
of all creation.

MADELEINE L'ENGLE

Sing a song of people
    Walking fast or slow;
People in the city,
    Up and down they go.

People on the sidewalk,
People on the bus;
People passing, passing,
In back and front of us.
People on the subway
Underneath the ground;
People riding taxis
Round and round and round.

People walking singly,
People in a crowd;
People saying nothing,
People talking loud.
People laughing, smiling,
Grumpy people too;
People who just hurry
And never look at you!

Sing a song of people
    Who like to come and go;
Sing of city people
    You see but never know!

LOIS LENSKI

Here's to thee,
Old apple-tree!
Stand fast root,
Bear well top,
Pray God send us
A youling crop!

Every twig
Apple big;
Every bough
Apple enow;
Hats full, caps full,
Fill quarter sacks full!
Holla, boys, holla!
Huzza!

ANONYMOUS

Tambourines!
Tambourines!
Tambourines!
To the glory of God!
Tambourines
To glory!

A gospel shout
And a gospel song:
Life is short
But God is long!

Tambourines!
Tambourines!
Tambourines!
To glory!

LANGSTON HUGHES

O our Mother the Earth, O our Father the Sky,
Your children are we, and with tired backs
We bring you the gifts you love.
Then weave for us a garment of brightness;
May the warp be the white light of morning,
May the weft be the red light of evening,
May the fringes be the falling rain,
May the border be the standing rainbow.
Thus weave for us a garment of brightness,
That we may walk fittingly where birds sing,
That we may walk fittingly where grass is green,
O our Mother the Earth, O our Father the Sky.

FROM THE TEWA INDIANS
OF NORTH AMERICA

The day is done;
The lamps are lit;
Woods-ward the birds are flown.
Shadows draw close –
Peace be unto this house.

The cloth is fair;
The food is set.
God's night draw near.
Quiet and love and peace
Be to this, our rest, our place.

ELIZABETH MADOX ROBERTS

God bless all those that I love;
God bless all those that love me;
God bless all those that love those that
    I love,
And all those that love those that
    love me.

FROM AN OLD NEW ENGLAND SAMPLER

Allah, my Lord,
eyes are at rest,
stars are setting,
hushed are the movements
of the birds in their nests.
The doors are locked,
Watched by guards,
but your door is open
to him who calls upon you.

ADD AL' AZIZ AL-DIRINI
ISLAMIC PRAYER

God bless the master of this house,
   God bless the mistress too,
And all the little children
   That round the table go.

ANONYMOUS

Sleep, sleep, my little one! The night is all wind and rain;
The meal has been wet by the raindrops
    and bent is the sugar cane;
O Giver who gives to the people, in safety my little son keep!
My little son with the headdress, sleep, sleep, sleep!

TRADITIONAL EAST AFRICAN
(translated by Holling C. Holling)

From ghoulies and ghosties,
Long-leggety beasties
And things that go bump in the night
Good Lord deliver us.

TRADITIONAL SCOTTISH

Creator of the world
Help us love one another,
Help us care for each other
As sister or brother,
That friendship may grow
From nation to nation.
Bring peace to our world
O Lord of Creation.

TRANSLATED FROM
JAPANESE